Maybe,

I Love Too Hard

This is a compilation of pieces from my previous published works. You will find pieces from the following books:

The Journey Through My Heart
I Was Never Broken Volume 1,2, and 3.
The Feels the Moon & My Soul
Hidden Gems
YoungNakedSoul
Self-Talks
Heal Inspire Love
Free Mind

This is a great collection for you to start reading if you haven't read any of my books. It gives you a dive into each book and the vibe. I wouldn't say these pieces are my greatest work, or my favorite, because each book is very special to me, and my growth as a person and a writer. I know these pieces will shed light on anyone who needs them at this current moment. I also added new pieces that fit perfectly with this collection.

I hope you enjoy the emotional ride, as always.

Maybe, I Love Too Hard

You're not **dumb** to *love someone with all your heart,*
To want someone who is *no good for you.*

People with good hearts have the most trouble
with this; we see the best in people and expect
them to see the same in us. You can't make
someone love you. That's why it's important to not
wait around for someone who won't ever grow
with you. For the ones who wake up one day and
decide they no longer love you, let them go. Let
them go the second they give you that sign.
Knowing they couldn't be straightforward from the
beginning. A reminder, no response doesn't mean
there's hope. There's no need to attach crazy ideas
that love will revisit like the first time you fell in
love with them. Don't let them come back, time and
time again, while they leave you without wonder.
You don't deserve to wait around for love; that's
unclear, **undecided,** and *gone.*

You put your all into someone you loved, you were clueless about why you did. When you love intensely, it can get the best of you, and not always in a good way. You let love become a weapon; you become blinded by it. You'll know the difference between the two kinds of love when you realize yourself loving them and not trying your hardest to prove that love. When it's real, they will feel it as much as you. There are ups and downs, but no one who truly loves you will ever hurt you and make you believe you're someone hard to love. People with big hearts let love not only be a good drug but also let it destroy them. If you never learned what love isn't, you could never appreciate what love is. You'll never understand the real if you can't compare the fake. Everything you go through in life is a lesson. We need to find the parts of us that are still hidden; we often learn something new about ourselves. You need to accept not everyone is meant for you. Some will only be out to hurt you because that's the role they were meant to play in your life, don't try and change that.

To the men who broke my heart

I'm thankful it was only a fracture, even though it felt like an eternity to heal. I carried the bruises with me like a warrior; I had to; my picture of love then was a battlefield. Your inconsistency was humiliating, but I kept clinging and hoping for reassurance. I'm very selective now; back then, I voluntarily chose pain if there was a chance it was linked to love. I let go of my morals when I became fluent in choosing empty promises. I hoarded the beautiful moments. My vision became blurry when my heart's language wasn't matched. My soft heart didn't deserve to be stained with your cheap version of love. I craved a connection so tender that you seemed to taint with your chaotic ways. Your conviction still haunts me, but the lessons are embedded deep inside me and attainable when I need them to resurface, to remind myself to never settle for the echoes of your cheap potential ever again.

A dose of manipulation

I was lost. I used my love as a weapon and sometimes a manipulation to be loved in return. I wanted to feel loved. I wanted to feel how good it felt to be in love. I tried to create it within a lot of the wrong ones. I tried to save and fix everyone while damaging myself. I couldn't recognize the real from the phony because I let myself be vulnerable and blinded by my need to be loved. I set up my heartbreak. I couldn't trust anyone; I let them get close only to push them away.

10 people I needed to let go of:

1. The one who manipulated me, belittled me.

2. The one I outgrew.

3. The one who outgrew me.

4. The one whose memory took up too much mental space.

5. The one good at faking.

6. The pettiness inside me.

7. The shy, timid, and fearful soul inside me.

8. The one who never accepted me.

9. The one who made me feel hard to love.

10. Everyone who couldn't embrace me wholeheartedly.

ROUTINE LOVE

I settled for struggle love because I thought the constant fight was worth it. I gave up some of my biggest dreams to be in the presence of someone I loved because I thought sacrifices needed to be made to survive it. I thought healing each other was the strongest commitment; until I was taken for granted and left stranded. *I settled for routine love* because I thought comfort meant security, but it came in the form of codependency. I settled for this stagnant relationship I couldn't afford to free myself of; the whirlpool of disaster I let it become because I thought love would be enough. I wish someone would have told me the love couldn't only be felt by me. I wouldn't have fought to be with someone who ended up a stranger.

FALL IN LOVE WITH YOURSELF

Fall in love with yourself. Fall in love with the intention to fall, but with the uncertainty of what is to come. Fall in love with chapters that are behind you, and the moments to come. Fall in love with the scars you hold, even if they can't be forgotten or forgiven. Fall in love with your flaws even if they can't be erased. Fall in love with your vulnerability, your wit, and your heart. Falling in love with your life is a form of self-care but loving the life you live is a form of self-love.

READ THIS BEFORE LOVING ME

If you're going to love me, know that it's not hard. I won't make you fight for my love, I will embrace you with complete openness; you will reside in my heart like the home you've craved. I will nurture you when you feel lovesick. I will be the friend you cry to, lean on, and always run to. I won't make you uncomfortable unless it's time to stand in your truth; my discomfort will only come in the form of helping your growth. I won't deceive you. I won't try to change you. I will always support you.

If you're going to love me, know that it may not always be easy. I am an intense lover, sometimes I may suffocate you. I'm an overthinker, extra TLC is recommended. I'm an empath, my emotions get the best of me; and get the worst of you, if you're not ready to embrace them. I don't think that makes me hard to love. I think it just means I was meant to be experienced differently. I think it means those who find me in this world were either meant to bring me love or bring themselves the experience they were missing within; both are a treasure.

Do me a favor,
stay away from me,
If you don't have good intentions.
I don't have it in me
any longer,
to give my love
to those who only abuse it.

Whether we become one,
I still have the most incredible memories of my life.
Thank you for giving me the chance,
to love you,
to experience a piece of life with you.
You have become my best friend,
I hope you know that.

I let go of people
I still love,
that's strength,
that's growth.

If you **push me away**,
I promise you,
you won't find me where you left me.
My heart's big,
but not big enough to deal with people
who decide to love me
when it's *convenient for them*.

A LETTER TO AN OLD FLAME

I loved you very much; I'm not sorry about that.
Back then, I'd say I was. But now, I thank you. I
thank you very much for showing me what love
isn't. Showing me what it's like to deal with
someone who never made my heart skip a beat but
only made it stop beating for you. I look back then,
and I see the girl I was vulnerable, kindhearted,
terrified of heartbreak, and in complete lust with
you. It wasn't until now I realized I never really
loved you. Because looking back, there wasn't
anything to love about you but the idea. I was in
love with loving you. I was in love with the
thought of giving my all to you, hoping it would
make you love me back. I was attached to the idea
of loving you; I forgot to love you. I see the signs
now, the signs I should have ran when I had the
chance. The times I always gave in when I should
have left. I put my heart out there to get destroyed,
and you chose to destroy me every time. I was
blinded; I didn't know our love wasn't conditioned.
My heart was confused. My heart never
understood why I kept letting someone like you in.
But I know now why I had to open my heart to
you. I understand why I needed to give you a piece

17

of me I'll never receive back. It's a piece I don't ever need back. I don't need the pain of getting hurt after putting my heart on the line for you. I don't need that piece of me back. You may savor that piece with you everywhere you go. Remember me for everything I was to you. The love I gave to you, the comfort I brought. The trust I had broken every time.

I want you to remember me for everything I was because you will never know who I am today. I suffered so long trying to end my journey with you; it was a blessing to let you go. You always came back; I would be a fool. I'll never forget the day I gave you my final goodbye. I always wondered how you felt at that moment, but I realized I don't care as I'm writing this. I don't care how I made you feel because you never cared to wonder how I felt when you chose you every time over me.

Maybe that's it... you chose yourself every time over me. Perhaps that's it... you chose yourself when I should have chosen myself.

Maybe that makes me angry.
Maybe it's anger I hold inside of me towards you.
Because...
I couldn't love myself enough to see right through you.

The most **toxic** and *destructive* kind of love is the kind of love that isn't reciprocated. The type of love you lose yourself trying to keep them together. When your heart is big, you find yourself attaching yourself to people who need saving, to people who are broken in hopes you can heal them. In hopes, you could be the one who shows them their worth. No amount of energy you put into this toxicity will ever be worth your sanity or your ability to give someone your heart that deserves to love you. We confuse love with lust a lot and attach love to almost everything in hopes of filling the void we've longed to fill within ourselves. Don't ever lose yourself trying to fight for "love" that only exists to you. Stop finding reasons to hold onto hopes that love might visit because you're sure they will love you with time. Some people don't deserve the love you give. You won't need to fight to make your love noticed; when you find your soul's match, you won't ever need to second guess that love because it's the kind of love that will be instantly reciprocated.

A LETTER TO THE LOVE I ALMOST HAD

I remember wondering what we could be. I became accustomed to my fantasy of us, I couldn't see the reality presented in front of me. So, I couldn't blame you for the tragedy my heart was left with for years to come after the loss of you. I couldn't blame you for not loving me the way I thought you could. I couldn't blame you for hiding the truth from me because I would have found a reason not to believe you. Instead, the lies kept me around. The mystery of what we could have been having me high, too high; I couldn't imagine coming down. I couldn't imagine being without you, and I didn't even have you.

I blamed you for many of the scars that came with our ending. Back then, when I was young and naïve, I blamed you for misleading me, you could have walked away once you saw the love bleed out of me for you, but you chose to hold me close and play me as your fool. I blame you for continuing to hurt me, as you had every moment to confess, we weren't meant to be, that I saw a future envisioned that you couldn't give me. I spent years giving you everything I could; I don't blame you for that.

I blame myself for trying to force something the universe kept taking away from me. I couldn't blame you for all the times I came back, hoping this time may be ours. So, I can't blame you for our tragedy; I can't even blame myself; we both played our roles. I was once bitter towards the thought of you; now, I'm aware of why I had to love you so deeply and why I had to lose you. The best thing about you, even though you couldn't love me, you showed me what love wasn't; you brought me the best gift, the road to self.

I was never meant to save you.
I was only meant to love you
until the universe decided
It was time for me to part ways.

I didn't deserve
to be ignored because of your bad day,
I didn't deserve
to be treated like a burden
because you couldn't
find your worth along the way.

A message to my trauma:

I said my goodbyes to the things I couldn't keep holding onto. I was tired of letting you tear me apart. I was exhausted trying to find ways to fill voids through souls knowing I could never build homes within broken walls and improper foundations. I was searching for someone to heal me, but the bandage never stuck. I wasn't aware I had to be my redemption. I felt hollow, echoed by sadness, and hidden in spaces I couldn't seek comfort. I created a bond with trauma, I became codependent on getting my heart broken. I became reckless with my heart when I held it hostage from growth. I thought since someone broke me, they deserved to compensate me for my loss. It was a messy game I played to be loved. I thrived in sadness; it was the only feeling that wasn't fleeting.

Transparent love

I want to thank you for loving me, even if it wasn't enough or the way I deserved. I needed your love, as intangible as it was, it brought tranquility before the storm. It helped me adore myself more. It highlighted the compassion I was lacking for myself. I was devoted to you, blindly stubborn... I was unstable and cruel to my own heart. It was almost like you were a sad song, one I kept overplaying because it ignited something in me... until you sucked all the tenderness out of me. I no longer wish to hit replay.

I'm not a *pitstop*
kind of love,
my heart is the destination.

Don't use "love" as an excuse to keep unwanted company around your soul. Don't use "love" as an excuse to fight for a connection that's outgrown you. Don't use "love" as an excuse to rebuild bonds that bandages never stuck to, the wound is still fresh. Don't use "love" as an excuse to be a doormat to someone who carelessly "missteps" and "doesn't mean to hurt you". Don't use "love" as an excuse to stay, when the only love you're fighting for is the love you're giving that was never returned. Don't keep accepting that form of love or you'll forever be a stranger to your own heart.

I've always been in my *soft era*.
A cold heart was never a match for my soft one.
Vulnerability is my superpower.
Sensitivity is my strong suit.
I'm always welcoming
more love, peace, and happiness.

I'm an *energy reader.*

The **fake love**
The fake spiritual persona
The fake disguises
You can't fake it with me.

Your energy meets me before you do.

If you aren't
watering your soul, **healing** your heart, or *nurturing*
your growth, I can't have you around me. I can
love you with all of me and still part ways if you
don't care enough to take care of yourself. That
kind of energy will only leave me drained.
Self-care is essential to me.

I'm all about giving **second chances**

Until there comes a time when you have no more chances left to give. Taking the same people back after the first time doesn't feel the same. The more you allow, the more they'll keep doing it. Sometimes we love the thought of love and attach it to someone because we want to love. It's hard to know when love's real. I don't believe in second chances when it comes to real pain, repeatedly. I believe it takes time to understand the pain you feel, which makes it hard to let go. You'll never let the one who's meant for you find you if you keep running back to them. The one thing about toxic people, they'll swear to love you but leave you and then want you back. They can't have you and everything else they want. You're hurting yourself more by sticking around than letting go.

To **love yourself**,

It takes a lot of heartbreak and losing people you thought you'd never live without. It causes you to lose yourself, realizing there's no one you need more than yourself. **Don't rush the process**; *don't set comfort* in places you need to work to be happy.

No more lost connections

I'm not interested in being **liked,** *understood,* or **accepted.** Those don't determine my worth. I live in a world filled with people who always try to make me into someone I don't recognize. I'm *not interested* in making any more **lost connections.**

PIECES OF ME

Parts of me still live in the past because those parts of me died when those stories did. Parts of me live in fear because the unknown is terrifying; knowing forever isn't promised. Parts of me live within old lovers because they took a piece of me with them that I'll never receive back; a piece of me I no longer needed. Parts of me are still with old friends because we outgrew our story and the love still exists; just in a different form now. Parts of me still haunt me, the parts I couldn't love enough and I couldn't make peace with; they still urge me to pay more attention and give extra care. Parts of me still fear what could happen because nothing good ever came until I lived through the heartache.

I deserve someone who hugs me tighter on my darker days. Someone who doesn't judge or suffocate me when I need a moment to breathe. Someone patient and tender when holding my heart in their hands. I deserve someone who doesn't mix pain with love and creates an unhealthy environment to grow; someone who can flourish with me. I deserve someone who sees my value and doesn't downplay my potential; someone who showers me with praise and celebrates me, endlessly. I deserve someone who will love me, shamelessly. Someone who vows to stand the rain, the anxious outbursts, and sorrowful days without a source because the sun will always shine again. Someone who brings a force with them—a light. I deserve someone who doesn't just love me, someone, who won't ever stop proving it. I deserve someone who brings me peace, someone who feels like home to me.

 I vow to be this person,
to be this deserving because I will be this love for myself, first.

Self-love is
shedding the old layers
to make room for who you are becoming.
It is a homecoming
to the healthiest version of you.

Not everything lost needs to be found.
Not everything you lose is a loss.
Some situations are meant to *free* you.
Some experiences are meant to *teach* you.
Let them.

Maybe right now your journey isn't about finding love; maybe it's about discovering yourself in every aspect before you step into the chapter of loving anyone or letting them love you. Maybe right now it's time to focus on what you have and not what you desire, but to plant the seeds for what you want and water it until it grows; and if it doesn't, don't give up, try a different direction. We focus on what we want and never focus on where our life is at this current moment. We forget this is exactly where we need to be. We forget there's so much to life because we latch onto what we don't have. We tend to live in the past and the future but never in the present moment. We take for granted the greatest moments because they're not what we expected, without realizing expectations kill every thing. Maybe your journey isn't where you want to be, but it's where you need to be, so embrace the ride.

If you push me away,
I won't be here
when you decide, I'm worth it.
I won't be here
when you decide, I'm the one.
My heart doesn't have
what it takes anymore,
to be an open house
to broken souls.
I was never an option,
I refuse to be treated
like I'm worthless.

No one will love you,
like I do.
My love hits differently.
There's something authentic about it,
but it doesn't mean it was for you
or it wasn't toxic.
My love only goes as far
as it's reciprocated.
I have this habit of holding on
when I need to let go,
to better myself,
to grow.

A LETTER TO AN OLD FLAME

I convinced myself I loved you through those years of wasted moments trying to make you mine. I was young and naïve, and you used that to play me, to get me where you wanted me. I let you ghost me and come back when you pleased because I was love drunk off the idea of what we could be. I let you live a double life because I was too blind to see clearly. The words you spoke had so much meaning until you never followed through. I waited, I prayed, and I had faith it could be us. I blamed myself for a lot of the times it didn't work out when it was your time to take the blame. I never understood why you'd waste your time if you didn't love me or if you didn't care. So, I kept trying to analyze a love that wasn't loved at all. More so, a love of convenience. You kept me around to make you feel good and then left me to wonder what could become. It was wrong the way you played my heart, but it never missed a beat. So, I always chose to stay. So, shame on me. Shame on me for letting you walk all over me. Shame on me for letting you get into the depths of my soul that no one has ever touched. Shame on me for putting up with your mind games. Shame on me for believing love would ever live within you. But, shame on you for always misleading me. Shame on you for always making me feel we had a chance. Shame on you for keeping me in your fantasy of what we could be; when you had every opportunity to set me free, you chose to let me dream. So, the day our chance finally presented, I took it, and it was nothing I dreamt of. It just brought me closer to accepting you are never good for me. It just got me closer to accepting there's someone else out there for me, someone better than who you could ever be.

Abandonment Issues

I hated being alone
more than a day,
but I often found myself
hiding away,
because I needed to be alone.
Abandonment issues,
when you feel the need to be close
because everyone you love
seems to drift away
just when you get close.
So,
I would chase
like it was a race
to keep them close.
I thought I needed
their presence to feel safe,
but the chase for their heart
costed me.
Those abandonment issues
were unhealthy attachments
to never face my trauma,
until I came face to face
with my demons.
I was chasing comfort in the people
who left me,
I abandoned myself.

Not everyone deserves
your unconditional love.
Sometimes your love needs
to be conditional,
under the terms
of being *reciprocated*.

Mirror talks

I don't understand why they couldn't see you. I
don't know why they couldn't feel the vibrations
your soul radiates; instead, they rather sympathize
with your flaws and dilute them until you're
begging to be set free of your insecurities. I don't
understand why they couldn't love you past your
physical curse. I don't know why you couldn't be
desired because something jeopardized their taste.

But you, you always saw them. You always felt
every fleeting moment. You always questioned
their intentions. You always caught every sign. You
also felt every stimulating moment. You weren't
biased; you even loved those who were broken.
You were often seen guilty for trying to mend
them, failing every time, you weren't their savior,
but they were your kryptonite.

They never deserved to feel you; that's why they
couldn't ever see you.

Healing can get dark,
but there's so much beauty
in the darkness

- *I said to the moon*

Thank you to the ones who love me:

I owe a piece of my growth to you. You faithfully stood by me when I was drifting, searching, and witnessing myself. You helped me bandage the wounds. You opened my view to something more than the illusion I had in rotation. You were the warmth I needed to soften. You kept loving me even at my worst, even when I couldn't. I just wanted to tell you that your love is inspiring and has saved me many tears.

I wore my heart
on my sleeve
like it was an open invitation
to break me.

Be with someone who is as transparent as you, someone who communicates through and doesn't ghost when they're upset, but also respects the boundaries of space needed to clear one's mental space. Someone who loves every fiber of your being. Someone who takes the time to listen without reacting. Someone who lets you reflect without judgment. Someone who supports without expecting the same effort, they do it because they believe in you. Someone who is effortlessly your chosen safe place. Someone who doesn't fear your past but takes the time to learn the broken parts of you, without the need to repair… but never repeats those patterns with you. Someone who loves you because of every imperfection. Be with someone who makes it easy to love them, after feeling so hard to love. I think everyone deserves to find that one person who makes all the difference.

I think everyone deserves a healthy love.

Narcissist Reflections

A narcissist will suck you for every good you have in you, they will convince you that you're no good... it's true. They will also have you questioning yourself and you end up developing toxic traits, you become right where they want you. When you free yourself from the hold they have over you, it's up to you to put in the work to heal and unlearn those patterns they placed on you. Letting yourself escape the pain and trauma will keep you in that dark place subconsciously, you won't see it but you will repeat these behaviors to everyone who comes in after. There's no such thing as a distraction for healing, you suppress and become a toxic risk to your mental health and everyone who loves you. It's not about finding love with someone opposite of what you've loved before... it's about healing the version of you that holds the trauma and pain that attracts the wrong ones. There's a difference between being trauma bonded with someone and having a bond with trauma. It's important to look deep inside because it all starts with you. If you forever run from the demons that haunt you, you will forever accept the love that only hurts you.

I owe myself an apology
for allowing fear and rejection
to make a monster out of me.

Falling in love with someone
you had no intention of falling for,
is the most beautiful kind of love.
No forcing chemistry,
or trying to save them.
Just a pure,
raw connection
created on its own.

You deserve a love that transcends as you both go through growing pains. A love that's emotionally intelligent, patiently holding you a safe space. The dynamic of lovers and friends. Someone who doesn't depreciate your softness, makes you feel hollow, or any hue of blue. **A love that heals**.

Soulmates:

A love that transcends the world's assumption of "romance" because it's deeply rooted in connecting on a soul level without attachments to a label.

A letter to anyone *learning* to **love themselves**

Self-love doesn't come easy; learning to love yourself is just as challenging as loving others but more intensely. Loving yourself is so important. Every company you keep until you do won't be fully conditioned. When you have people around who help you grow, the ones who help you find you, those are the ones you keep around. You need to surround yourself with those who want to see you win just as much as you do. The more you involve yourself with people who half love you, fake love you, and give you conditional love, the further away you will feel from yourself. You need to get rid of the people who don't want to see you win. Get rid of those who **love you in the dark** while supporting people they hate in public.

    This is not the generation of people with pure hearts. People would rather waste time giving you fake love while letting you give them your heart. Don't let these people in your life for any reason; they'll make your journey a longer road. It's essential to protect your aura from people who drain your energy and heart from loving people with good hearts. Don't let the demons of your journey bring you to fear in accepting the truth in who you are, where you want to be, and where you're at now. Trust the energy you give, and you will receive that exact in return. Love the ones who love you back unconditionally. Keep the real ones close while you let the ones who drown your soul of sadness and hatred in the dark. Let them go. Be who you want to be. Don't let anyone tell you who you should be; the way you wear your heart on your sleeve is so beautiful.

    I promise **falling in love with yourself** is just as beautiful, while having people who love you close is like having the *whole moon in your hands*, incredible.

I **wanted** you,
at the time,
I thought I needed you,
I was **blinded** by what I thought love was
and it was making me a fool.

Losing someone is a complex part of life.

It doesn't matter how; it will hurt. The worst part about letting go is you'll still love them. It's crazy how our hearts can continue loving someone who only brings pain. You were meant to love everyone who walked in your life; it's impossible to analyze every connection you created, but when it's over, you'll feel it. There's nothing that will ease the pain; what's gone is gone. Don't drown yourself in pain that no longer serves its purpose. The longer you hold onto it, the longer you'll go without finding it again.

They don't define your beauty

You were beautiful before them, while you were with them, and now. They don't define your beauty. Your beauty is deeper than what meets the eye. Think about your heart, how you love, and how you show that love openly. That's your **authentic** beauty, *don't let anyone take that from you.*

Maybe, I Love Too Hard

I don't have it in me,
to do people how they do me.
I'm still trying to understand,
If it's my biggest strength
or my biggest weakness.

I let go of people
I wanted to keep around forever.
To me,
that's become my biggest **strength**.
If you know me,
you know my heart's big
and my love is *unconditional*.
If I let you go,
It was for reasons
that don't need explanation,
other than it wasn't me,
It was you.

Toxic people are dangerous.
You'll love them
with all your heart.
Without knowing,
your heart is breaking
because of **them.**

Finding yourself is the biggest struggle; loving yourself is incredibly hard. Yet loving others, saving others, and being the one savior is easy. We put our all into someone else, in hopes of filling *the void* we long to find in ourselves.

Maybe, I Love Too Hard

Please come whole if you plan to love me
I don't have what it takes,
to build a home
that's fitting for us two.
That's not love.

Please don't love me
if you don't possess the ability,
to love me to my core.
I don't have what it takes to teach you,
that's not fair to me.

Please don't stay in my life
just to lead me to a place of disappointment.
Don't allow me to sacrifice my worth
to save us,
when you know there's no rescuing us.

Please don't shatter my fragile heart
In a heartbeat
because you couldn't be bothered to be real.
Be honest with me.

Please don't love anyone
before you love yourself.
No one deserves to forget their worth
because the wrath of your selfish uses,
wait until you possess the power
to love what's within.
Don't do for love, what you cannot do.

PROMISES

I promise to stop trying to fit into spaces I don't belong.

I promise to not over-compensate my love until it becomes loss.

I promise to never stay where I'm not loved.

I promise to remember my worth every time it's threatened, and all the time because **I AM ENOUGH**.

I promise to protect my heart at all costs.

I promise to seclude my soul from those who come to toy and destroy, to keep it sacred.

I promise to always sing the praise of my successes, to remind myself of every blessing.

I promise not to fall victim to old patterns, faces, or feelings.

I promise to only visit the past in reflections, dwelling is off-limits.

I promise to not allow temporary emotions to become permanent feelings.

I promise to always give myself the time, patience, and love I deserve.

SORROW OUTTAKES

Sadness was the soundtrack of my story for so long, I put my happiness on pause. I became a doormat to being who everyone else needed. Someone who was once so pure. I thrived in chaos; I made a home in people who ended up leaving me. I gained comfort from temporary emotions because I feared real love. I didn't fear how it would feel. I feared I wouldn't be worthy enough—so I would immediately ruin it. I was fixated on saving something I never experienced. There was no proof the love I was chasing was a sure thing.

You're not obligated to keep opening the door for those who closed it on you and left you behind. You feel the need to keep circling back because they keep spinning back around. Unexpected returns are not déjà vu, they're reborn temptations to your fatal attraction.

- *Lessons of love*

Our time expired years ago. Our connection still
lingers in my heart. My love for you still exists.
That's why it will never not hurt to be without you.
Even though we rekindled, forgiven, and grew.
We're far from what we once knew. We're
strangers.

I miss you,
I miss my best friend

Some people
will never love you
the way you need to be loved,
because they haven't yet
loved themselves in that capacity.

Hostage

You never deserved me
In any way
shape
or form,
you never deserved to know me
from the depths of my soul
to every beat of my heart,
but I let you,
I let you.
For far too long
I replayed this song
hoping the lyrics changed,
that our story could somehow transform
so, I'm no longer trapped
In the force of your possession
and I could somehow
break out of your prison.

To the woman I loved:

I wasn't ready for your love, I admit it. I was timid at the thought of letting myself close. I didn't know what it would be like to open myself to you. I built this wall that turned into a whole space; I trapped myself deep inside it. Your essence was mesmerizing; I felt it as soon as we locked eyes. Your aura was as comforting as the waves hitting the ocean under the moon. Your soul was wild but tamed when your soft heart came into play. Being free was the melody you set in your harmonic ways. I adored you. I became fearless after losing you; I couldn't take the chance of being afraid to ever let someone love me as I did you. The rush I still get from thinking of you, the canvas I painted of you, the smile that captivated me way back then, it's all faded into this forsaken place in my soul. I need you to know; that I will love you endlessly; I just placed you there alone. You're a void I don't ever want to fill.

I realized,
communication didn't matter
If you couldn't comprehend.
The slightest misunderstanding
could be an impulse to abandon
and ghost.

- *Silence seemed like the high road*

<u>Broken</u>

I broke the moment
I heard the news,
you were gone.
I broke
the moment I felt your soul
and not your touch.
I still yearn for you to be whole.

Just because
you brought me pain,
I don't wish the same for you.
I don't want the same
karma coming for me
that's coming for you.

<u>Vows</u>

I won't ever let a love
like ours go,
or die.
I will live in;
nourish it,
cherish it,
and forever keep it alive.
For once,
I feel alive,
I owe that to you.
I'm whole from the love
I give myself,
and that missing piece,
the one
that fits with you.

Maybe, I Love Too Hard

My soul craves
a different kind of love,
the kind you give me.
The spontaneous,
welcome home kind of love,
a love I never felt before,
a love greater
then any kind I experienced,
your love is security,
your love is special.

Being with you,
felt like
I was surrounded
by broken clocks.

-   *a lot of wasted time*

The past is a storage space
we often forget to erase
we have unlimited space
when it comes to memories
ones we hold onto
In hopes to relive
except we revive an open wound
we never patched up.
So we continue
to love, heal, save, and fix
The broken
because we feel the need
to rewrite history
with this obsession
to relive a moment twice.
We chase
everything wrong for us
In hopes
to feel what once was.

THE PAST IS A DANGEROUS PLACE

BEFORE YOU GO TO BED

Pray for the ones you love and the ones you left behind. Pray for your health, your heart, and your happiness. No matter how crazy your day was, always take the time to pray for what you're most thankful for and the dark that became light.

Normalize letting people go
when it's no longer healthy,
not everything is worth fighting for.

One of the hardest things
I had to learn was **patience**,
to stop expecting everyone
to have the same mindset as I do.
To not hold everyone
to a high standard as I hold myself.

You won't always get that apology you're owed. You won't always get the closure you need. You won't always be felt and understood when it comes to your feelings. How you feel is valid but sometimes people don't understand they hurt you even if the proof is right in front of them. They will deny it because they don't view it the same as you, and that's okay. You don't need an apology or closure from someone who can't admit to the pain they caused you. You will heal and grow regardless. Be patient and embody how you feel because it's real. Don't let their manipulation change that.

We stay because we love hard. We put our hearts all in and there's no taking the love back. We manipulate our hearts to believe if we felt love, it was. We're taught to hold anyone close who made us feel something. When the same comfort they gave felt like home. We condition our hearts to believe we need their love since we've been dependent on it... we didn't once think it could be possible to live without it. We stay in hopes they change their heart and one day come back to us. We stay for the simple reason we love hard, making it hard to be loved in return knowing our worth is far more than what we're accepting... yet we consume less because we don't believe we're good enough.

A healthy love will never come from trust issues, old patterns, and suppressed pain. True love will never look into your eyes and lie. Real love will never open your soul without the intention of bringing peace and a place called home.

My Apologies

I'm sorry I wasn't enough for you, but I tried to be in every way it counts. I'm sorry you couldn't see my gift, my potential until you were threatened by someone who did. I'm sorry you took for granted a heart that was never broken, but a little damaged-which always balanced the scales. I'm sorry you couldn't find yourself so you gaslight your way through me. You broke me down and convinced me I was already broken, so me being the bad guy worked in your favor. You were never good at accountability or communication, which you realized once the clock ran out of time... our time. I'm not sorry about it, it brought me a greater lesson than any heartbreak ever could. How could I be sorry about a love that stayed consistent, a heart unmatched, and a soul yearning? I couldn't... you should be sorry for never cherishing those things.

Some *heartbreaks*
you never truly recover from.
You will heal,
and you will move on.
It will just **linger** in your heart forever.

When you love someone, you love them. Your whole soul loves them without thinking twice. It doesn't matter the relationship, **love is love**, and the people you love will be important in your life. Just like you were meant to meet people, you were meant to tell someone you thought you'd never need to let go. There are many paths out there; some people can't decide which road to take, and when they do, you may not take the same one. Don't let anyone make you feel the way you choose to grow is wrong, and who you are is someone unfamiliar. No one can identify you as someone you're not. Who you are will always be authentic when you give your heart, especially to people who only give their time.

Accept the *good* in **goodbyes**
Like you appreciate the first glace,
Both tie into *how you find yourself.*

The thing about people with **good hearts**,

we care too much.
We get upset over the little things
because everything we feel is real.
I've accepted,
I can't change what's not meant to be
, and my heart never will change.
I just trust **karma** to do its thing.

The **pain** will always make you feel like nothing.

It takes time to heal wounds that are still fresh. It doesn't matter how long it lasted; if you have a good heart, the way you love will always feel difficult, and the pain will always feel unbearable. *You must let yourself feel everything*, and know; you can either feel the heartache forever or try to find **happiness** in places it does exist.

I want to be loved in a way
It won't *hurt*
and I won't need to worry.
Because I,
will be everything I am
and that will be **enough**.

Selfish

From giving all of me,
to always love more.
I don't regret it
but there's no chance
you'd catch me a second time
giving all of me
to someone,
who took more than they could give.

I can't believe I ever thought
loving myself was *selfish*.

On this battlefield, one I created for myself trying to make you feel me. I stand here without any armor or shield to protect me. I took my best shot and it misfired. I should have spent more time learning how to be deserving instead of teaching you to love me. I should have spent more time protecting myself instead of waiting for you to validate me. I should have listened to your ultimatums and recognized your red flags instead of trying to fight for a bond that was conditional, unfair, and misconstrued. I should have guarded my heart instead of giving you a dozen second chances to ruin me.

You will always be enough for the right person. The person who doesn't allow you to settle, but encourages you to realize your potential. The person who stands by and watches you bloom — who pours into your cup when you're running low, to fuel the self-love in you. You will always be enough for the person who understands your heartache, acknowledges your scars, and sympathizes with your losses. A person who doesn't hinder your recovery or make you feel ashamed of your past. The person who is inspired by your dreams and ambitions — who doesn't silence your fears, but instead, allows them to have enough room to grow into triumphs. The person who creates a space for you to be your authentic self without trying to dim down your emotions, ego, or vision. The person who will also check you if you need realignment. You will always be enough for the person who chooses you. The person who is the right amount of love, inspiration, and refuge you need. You will always be enough for the right person, once you believe you are deserving of it.

I once thought *love*
was the cure for loneliness,
until I fell in love with someone
who made me feel lonely.

TAKE YOUR BEST SHOT

Handle me with care. Be gentle with my heart. Don't make this another heartbreak on my list of regrets. I won't come for revenge but karma will pay your dues. It will humble you. Please, know the risks before taking my heart for a ride you can't see through. *Don't love me if you don't plan to love your hardest.*

My love language is creating a sanctuary you can come to whenever you feel the need to escape. I will be your safe place to fall. I will be your shield when you're at war. I will love you with all of my will. *I just hope you love me enough,* to not allow me to deprive myself of the same love I give you.

SURE THING

Falling in love with you was easy, there was nothing complex about the way you were ready to embrace me. I fell in love with the way you met me halfway; no pieces to pick up, no ulterior motives. You were ready to love me with your heart open and your soul naked. You walked into my life when I was discovering who I want to become. I was setting boundaries. I was breaking bridges. I was building foundations. I was seeking forgiveness. I was choosing me. I was searching for peace, and I found you, someone who brought the softest touch to my heart and ignited my soul. I knew at that moment—no storm could destroy, no darkness could diminish and our love was a sure thing.

I feared comfort
the moment I realized,
I settled because it was familiar
not because it made me happy.

Teach people how to treat and love you by leading the way with the way you talk to yourself, treat yourself, and embrace yourself with the love you want returned. Allowing people to walk all over you without the boundaries placed and the ability to know what you deserve will only place you into a pattern of destructive love. Be the reflection of the love you want. The love you deserve will only come in the form of what you accept.

5 WAYS TO HAVE A HEALTHY RELATIONSHIP WITH MYSELF:

1. *To treat myself* with grace and shower myself with patience. I deserve the same kindness I give.

2. *To listen* to my inner voice when it's uncomfortable. To never overlook, overthink, or overshare until I'm tired.

3. *Have self-talks* every time I need to be inspired. Speak positive affirmations when I'm struggling to see myself through the darkest moments.

4. *To never dismiss* my goals or desires — to indulge but to stand in my power. To always speak my truth and never silence my voice.

5. *To love myself* like I would love someone else — I deserve the same kind of effort.

Sometimes we *over-love*
when it's time to outgrow.

I'm living proof that *fighting for love*
doesn't always get you love, instead,
it gives you perspective,
a change in direction,
and the capability to let go when it's time.

"When do you know it's time to let someone go"

When I gave all of me,
to the point there was no more to give.
When they didn't question
when I became distant.
All the chasing
trying to prove my love.
When they decided not to chase me back.

Everyone you love in your life
should be a safe space,
not more stress that makes you worry,
or another battle you need to overcome.

Taking accountability is how you take control of your life. Knowing what you did wrong and correcting yourself is the highest form of *self-love*.

Start *your healing* first,
So others don't need to heal from you.
So, when someone tries to love you,
You let them.

You are someone's **favorite person**. The way you light up every room you walk into, the way you laugh with your entire face. Your ability to make every problem disappear when you're near. You don't realize the importance you bring to everyone around you. How incredible you are, being authentically you.

One of the scariest things in this world to experience is that someone can *love the idea of you*, and not even love you at all.

There's no hate in my heart for anyone. I don't have the *cold heart* to dismiss anyone that's never done anything to me, or even the ones who have. I only uplift and realign my energy to keep my intentions and heart pure.

My heart, intentions, and soul will always stay **pure**. The version of me you get will always be the outcome of how you treat me.

No longer matching energy, I'm maintaining my own. You either meet me where I'm at or not at all. I'm not going to dim myself down to meet you at a place I've grown from. *I wish you the best,* though.

I used to meet people halfway, now it's either, *meet me where I'm at* or leave me be. I don't have time to nurture a connection that will never grow.

No superpowers

I attracted broken souls so much
I thought it was my calling
to save, fix
and heal them.
I thought if I could,
they would love me.
I caught myself
drowning in their trauma,
I ended up almost broken
trying to mend them together.

Darkest Hour

I know I hurt you in the crossfire to save myself. I acknowledge that pain. I loved you through your darkest hour; you brought me to mine. Have you admitted why you couldn't save me, and I needed to save myself? The reckoning that became of us only hurt more, holding on. The pain we endured being entangled together made us feel like we needed each other. So, It hurt like hell for you when you realized I didn't need you. That your manipulative ways couldn't trap me. That your call for help didn't awake my savior complex. I'm done trying to save you when you didn't care to be; you only cared about ruining me.

Your unresolved trauma
will end up hurting everyone,
 including you
in the crossfire.
When you try and love them
with a broken heart.

The only way
I'll be teaching someone
how to love me,
is by showing them how I love and treat myself,
providing my love languages.
I won't be providing
chance after chance
because *you wouldn't read the open book I am.*

I pushed people away
so, they couldn't hurt me.
I pushed people away
and expected them to fight for me.
I tried to prove my love
by saving and fixing
every broken soul
so that they would love me.
I was blaming love
when it was me,

- *I was chasing everything but peace.*

Gravity

I was soul-searching when I found you. Your heart's language was like a vacation to my soul. Your tenderness was a breath of fresh air. You craved me in ways I always praised. Every part of me I tamed and held hostage, I set free. You never shamed me for not being whole, but you didn't feel the need to save me. The force that led me to you, I never questioned it; it's the closest to the moon I've ever been. You're the reflection of all the good I am. It's when I stopped trying to force my story, I discovered you. You are the definition of my soul's twin.

I *genuinely* fell for someone I didn't see coming. I was on the road to self-discovery when I found my best friend. I wasn't searching to be loved; I was growing and finding my peace. It's like my prayers were finally answered; my sanctuary was complete.

A soulmate

I fell in love with souls, many
not even romantically
an undeniable connection
embedded in the stars,
we aligned
a friendship created from the scars,
our secrets unleashed,
the freedom of comfort
in the darkest times turned to light,
like the moon at night
they all brought beauty to my life,
even if it was just a spark
or a flame,
our fate was written.
I'm so happy we collided
even if our story can't be forgiven.

If I could retrace our love
And take back the compromises I made
To be in sync with you
I would, in a heartbeat.

You poisoned me,
I rejected every antidote
You injected into me
Gaslighting and manipulation
Your spell of choice.

This time,
I'll cast the spell,

- *No more conditional traits*

I Was Broken

I'm not sure why I wanted to safe keep every soul in distress. I'm not entirely convinced it was because I made myself accessible to them. I do have theories. I think the need to sympathize wasn't enough, so I overprioritized them. I pled guilty to a crime I didn't commit. So, here I was cleansing a soul I had no business fixing. I jeopardized my happiness at the cost of them not feeling pain. I wanted to spare those layers they were going to shed, that disturbing pain of heartbreak. I wanted to be the hero this time; I was tired of being the victim. I wanted to feel purpose. I didn't for one moment wish ever to fade away from the puzzle I was putting together of my own. It was easier to love them than unpack the haunting pain I buried. I don't know why it was lighter to love the broken. Maybe it was a reflection of myself. Perhaps because I vowed to love myself, and I let myself down. Perhaps I was afraid to admit I was broken too.

Self-accountability

I volunteered as tribute
for the wreckage of my life
I made a mess of.
To the broken, the fragile, and the hurting:

1. I should have loved you with more empathy and less shame.

2. I should have watered your roots with reassurance and less tragedy.

3. I should have kept you safe with consistency and less nostalgia.

4. I should have had the courage to heal you without hurting you.

5. I should have told you your home will never be found in anyone but you; maybe you wouldn't be a home to vacant souls.

6. I should have saved you, but without the aching pain that touched you, you wouldn't see the magic in you, let alone believe it to be true.

My condolences

To anyone who lost me, to anyone I set free. I was tired of shrinking myself to your conflicted and confusing possession of who you wanted me to be. I was exhausted trying to worship something I envisioned, something that never bloomed. I was depleted trying to feel your hues, but all I felt were the blues. My condolences to you for never seeing me for the majestic view I was; you just saw the reflection of you.

Self-destruction

I had my heart broken
the same way I broke hearts.
I manipulated myself
the same way I let myself be used.
I sat and waited
for the universe to align me
perfectly with the one.
I passed up some
for the wrong ones
I wrecked some
for the broken ones
I wanted to prove my love,
I wanted to be loved
truly, madly, deeply
I couldn't grasp
I was the broken one
and my path of destruction
brought me closer
to the shattered ones.

The love I planted in everyone else
I used to envy
until it didn't bloom.

I planted that same love
within me
and it thrived.

my garden consists of reassurance and softness

- *the key was always patience*

I found comfort in lonely nights,
my temptation with pain,
rejection and adaptation.
I forced romance often.
In my defense,
I had no clue what love was
so, an ice box for a heart
felt like the best defense mechanism.
Sorrow was the melody of my soul

- *and I was okay with it*

One of the hardest things to digest was to understand I could love someone, but I couldn't save, fix, or heal them. I could only stand by them, inspire them, and always do right by them.

My prayer,

I give myself permission to let go of everything keeping ties to me, so I can make room for what's meant for me, to align with me. I give myself permission to allow them in without the extra guard. I give myself permission to love and be loved the way I deserve, not the love I conditioned myself to believe, or I settled to make work. I give myself permission to set boundaries when needed, even within relationships with those I love most. I give myself permission to take care of home first, of myself. I give myself permission to plant seeds in areas of my life, in relationships, and my dreams. I will water them. I will refill the cup every time it's needed. I give myself permission to grow, be happy, and go for everything I want. I give myself permission to be free.

I know someone loved me . . .

When they didn't make me feel like I needed to compromise my brokenness with their wholeness, they accepted I was a work in progress. I didn't need to change or alter myself to be seen, heard, or understood. My passions didn't intimidate them. Instead, they clapped and celebrated me like I was their dream. They felt me, and when they couldn't, they gave me the space I needed to breathe. They brought patience, peace, and bliss. I know someone loved me when they loved me in my love language, not theirs.

There's no real love
In someone
who breaks your heart,
over and over
and watches you pick up the pieces.

Temporary love

I never loved the same way twice. To inner stand, this took a lot of digging and forgiveness. It took a lot of acknowledging I wasn't always the victim, but it also wasn't always my love that was tainted. I vowed to never love the same once my heart was abandoned and evaded misery. I was transparent to the heartbreak; I knew the only cure would be to find a harmony in tune... repeating the same old song would only bring a melody of chaos and symbolize how broken I would always end up. Loving the same would only burden me, I couldn't keep letting everyone get the best parts of me. Everyone who ignited a fire in me didn't deserve to be my endgame, some were only a flame.

No one meant for me
ever came
twice in this lifetime.

Sensitivity

If it's one thing I wish to be remembered for, it's for the souls I touched and left a mark on, even if it was for a fleeting moment. I want to be remembered for the way I love. I always make sure I show up when it's needed and check up when there's some distance. I always make sure everyone I love knows how much they're loved and how much I love them. I think that memory stays the longest.

You deserve

You deserve a love that doesn't force you to leave behind the things and people you love. You deserve a love that comes with conditions but is based on the foundation and boundaries you set. You deserve a love that isn't belittling, that never makes you question or lose your worth. You deserve a love that finds and embraces you. A love you don't need to save or make excuses for. You deserve a love that comes with no ulterior motives.

I genuinely fell for someone when I walked away from what no longer fed my soul. I left the baggage behind and they discovered me. They sparked my life with their light and made all the difference. I wasn't searching for them, I was pursuing peace. I was loving myself. Sometimes you just need to be patient and focus on yourself and the right ones will fall into your life and choose you.

It's not a **loss** *anymore, to me,*
when someone decides
to walk out of my life.
It's a loss to them,
having to remember me
for everything I am,
knowing they chose to let me go.

IN CASE YOU FORGOT:

You deserve to love yourself
with the same kind of love,
you give to everyone else.

If I like you,
You'll know. I don't vibe with everyone.
It's hard for me to make friends. I'm so distant. If I
enjoy your company or just you in general… you
mean something; *not everyone gets that side of me.*

The way I love will always be intense.
You will always feel my love.
Regardless of the time that passed,
you will never forget how my love felt.
Knowing I loved with all of me,
even when I couldn't love myself,
to me, *that's my beauty*.

JUNE 7, 2018
1:26 A.M.

I've been obsessed with saving people my whole
life, friends, and relationships. I always wanted
everyone to know my love was real and that my
passion was strong enough to heal whatever hurt
them. I always wanted to be loved in return, the
exact way I loved. Sometimes I let my guard down
when it came to people loving me back… just a bit
of love I ran with, and that's where I always went
wrong. I've been doing love wrong. I always loved
the same unconditionally. I had my fair share of
disappointments, which ended up my fault in the
end, but mistakes are lessons to learn from, right?

Love is such a big word.
I learned that love is a scary place to be if you're
not exactly sure you want to be there. It's crazy to
know how crazy I was in love back then and how
it's not one of my biggest fears. Because I've given
someone all of me, loved them with my whole
heart, and things still didn't work. I fear real love
because I'm terrified to know how it will feel… I'm
frightened to hurt the one I love because I've
already done that once.

APRIL 16, 2021
5:39 PM

I usually don't wish the worst on anyone; I still don't. I hope you feel how you made me feel and never repeat it for anyone else who decides to love you.

Don't let old flames
think it's possible to light new ways,
they will always
find new ways to burn you out.

I watched someone I loved,
love someone else
and I thought that was the lowest
I could ever feel.
until I realized,
they never belonged to me,
I was fantasizing about a love
that was one-sided,
and only felt by me.
I created my own heartbreak.

I don't only read the room,
I can feel it too,
and sometimes,
it's too much to handle.
It's a lot of energy taken from me
I let others' emotions affect me.
It's my nature
to try and save, heal,
and love the broken.
It hits too close to home.

I just wanted my love to be cherished.

You want to be loved,
so you give them a chance
but you end up
emptier than you were before.

Don't sacrifice your worth
for a chance to be loved.

I pray you see
It was best to set you free,
there wasn't happiness in we.

I'VE BEEN TO MY DARKEST PLACE

I know how hard it was to pull myself out of it. It takes a different kind of strength and a lot of patience. I'm praying for everyone at their darkest, and that doesn't talk about it. You're not alone; I hope you know that. You will make it through.

Self-love
will always be
the love that saves you.

TO EVERYONE I ONCE LOVED

I'm sorry for what I couldn't give you.
I'm sorry we couldn't make it, but you're worthy
and have great value. You're loveable. It's just time,
the universe, and the stars weren't aligned for us.
I hope you understand that.

Stop letting yourself go unappreciated
you deserve so much more
then to be someone's second best.

Our time expired.
Our connection will always be cherished.
I will always love you,
but I don't need to keep you in my life to do so.

I'm big on forgiveness,
I will forgive you
even after you almost ruined me.
Don't get it twisted,
It doesn't guarantee you a place in my life.

One thing we always get wrong,
trying to relive a moment
that was only meant
to be felt once.

One of the worst things
I put myself through,
was trying to fit into a crowd
when I already outgrew the environment.

I don't crave another presence at this moment,
I crave peace of mind.

Love is like a rollercoaster,
It looks fun,
but when you're on it,
It can be scary
and dangerous,
that's the risk I took loving you.

Healing from Someone You Still Love

I'm sorry it came down to which was more important, trying to make you love me or saving my entire being from becoming lost. I'm sorry for leaving you when I promised I would never. I'm sorry I broke so many promises. I'm sorry my growth scared you, and your eyes saw it as change. I'm sorry you couldn't understand the difference but always wanted different. I'm sorry you didn't love yourself the way you wanted, so you chose to use my heart for your burdens. I'm sorry you saw me as someone who could be without you, so you chose to push me in that direction. I'm sorry you couldn't find who you were, so you created who you wanted to be, and in the end, you never felt whole. I'm sorry I couldn't love you the way you hoped I could. I'm sorry you demanded so much but never thought what I gave was enough. I'm sorry I couldn't be the friend you wanted me to be. I'm sorry I need to love you from afar. I'm sorry the love we once shared became toxic to us. I'm sorry my soul won't ever get to rest without you. I'm sorry I loved you even when you didn't deserve it. I'm sorry I still do. Healing from someone you still love, it's crazy; after all this time, there's always love in my heart for you. But when I noticed your absence brought me peace, I knew one thing for sure; I wasn't sorry for choosing me.

It's not their job to heal me,
they shouldn't need to do time
for someone else's crime.
It's hard to love someone else
without the word **pain**
crossing every line
and the word *trust*
being erased from my mind.

Not everyone is meant for you,

There will be some who will only hurt you because that's the role they were meant to play in your life. So don't try to rewrite the story and change it.

Loving people who *don't deserve* your love will only **drown you in darkness**.

"What you *convinced* your **heart** was **real**."

While you focus on who you left behind or trying to leave behind, there's someone out there waiting to find you, while you're giving your love to someone who doesn't deserve it. Find *the love that feeds your soul*, not the version of the love you convinced your heart was genuine.

It's crazy,
you were raised to love people closely
and suddenly,
you grow up to learn
not *everyone*
was raised like you.
Some make it hard
to love them,
so **you end up**
loving them from afar.

"I want to breathe"

The **past** that haunts me,
the past that needs to die.
I don't want the memories,
let them die,
let them leave.
I want to forget them,
I want to breathe.

I will be the person I am, and if someone doesn't like me, they can forget me. If someone can't love me the way I want to be loved, in better words, the way I deserve to be loved, *I refuse to give my heart away.* No matter how long it takes, I won't let anything break me, every obstacle I will get through. Being happy with myself is the key to it all. I will no longer cry over what's not mine and instead be happy about the things I have. The universe took people and things out of my life for a reason. Not many can say they deserve the best because we all accept the things we think we deserve.

Life is too hard to understand; it's also too short to analyze. Don't spend too much time on something you know might never last, but don't give up on something if you believe in your heart is real. Accept that people change, things change, and sometimes nothing stays the same. Sometimes you need to let go. So many people don't know who they are, but **I've grown to understand me.**

There's *no shame in my love*
No shame in my heart
for the ones I lost.
I have no shame
for the ones *who left me to pick up the pieces.*
Each piece
led me to where I am today.
I thank you,
from the bottom of my heart,
for helping me find myself.
But do me a favor,
stay away from me.

Don't settle for what you think you deserve, don't just **settle for love**. Love isn't waking up one day, and the one you love doesn't love you anymore; that's far from love. When you love someone that intimately, you will feel it forever; in this story, forever does exist. Love will always be there, and if they say it wasn't, it never was. You can't wake up and not love someone anymore, but it's possible to outgrow people, change happens, but that love will always remain. You will meet people throughout your life that you will believe you love but won't love. If you ever woke up and thought it could be possible not to love them, it's not love you feel. **People with big hearts** always get confused; that's why it's vital to protect your heart from those who want you when they want you, then get rid of you when they don't need you. It's easy for them, but a person like you, with a big heart, *will scar your heart forever*.

There's nothing *wrong with your heart*,
Sometimes it doesn't understand the **first** time.

Find what makes you **happy**,
Make it your life.
Don't ever let go of anything
that *fills your soul*
or what makes you feel **alive**.

A message to a **lost** soul:

Don't worry why you haven't got to where you want to be already got to where you are. You can't expect to get everything you dreamed of without working for it. So do whatever you need to accomplish that dream. Some days will be more stressful than others, and some weeks will take forever to end. Some may pass so quickly that you won't remember every detail.
Life is crazy; it's also exciting.
You are life; you are **free**.
You deserve everything you set your mind to and let your heart make your biggest dreams come true.
Don't ever get comfortable but always have the comfort you will make it and always find a way. As lost as you may feel now, you'll realize that you always knew who you were; you were just too comfortable and never pushed yourself to your entire self.
You are like *the moon in the night sky*, **beautiful** and unreadable. There's nothing wrong with being a **mystery** to the world *if you never lose yourself.*

You deserve someone honest with you, who will tell you how they feel. Not someone who will wait for you to find out, then try picking up the pieces; that's not love. Love isn't waking up one day and finding out the one you love doesn't love you anymore.

Protect your heart.

If someone shares their **dreams, secrets,** and *fears* with you. Please don't use it against them when you're no longer in good company. They loved you enough to tell you the deepest and rawest parts they didn't share with the world.
They found comfort in you.

You **needed** me,
More than I needed you.
I gave all of me for your need,
Yet I'm the **damaged** one.
The one who's always made out to be
The lost one.

Under no obligation was *I meant to fix you,*
that didn't mean I didn't try.
I found myself almost **broken**
trying to mend together
what *wasn't my heartache to recover.*

It's always a choice,
you either *grow together*,
or you **outgrow** them.

My **intuition** has always brought light to every situation. Being able to sense the outcome of someone's actions before they even show me. Always trust every vibe you get; there's too much real love out there to be wasting your time on someone who only *loves you in the dark*.

You're **not hard to love**,
You just don't love with limitations.
You love with all your soul or not at all.
Don't take half love
from the ones *you give your whole heart* to.

You taught me —
infatuation is a phase
chemistry can burn out
connections can fade

You taught me —
love can be platonic
love can be demonic
love can be euphoric

You taught me —
everything is disposable
forever isn't forever
who we once were, isn't who we become

You taught me —
the most beautiful things can turn toxic.
Wasted time doesn't exist,
it's worth every moment spent.

You were a **teacher**
You were a teammate
You were a soulmate

If there's one thing I took from our connection, it's the
ability to always love my hardest even when I didn't
know if it would be reciprocated. *Life is most beautiful
when you expect the unexpected*, you can't be disappointed.

My *light*, you envied.
It threatened you
because you feared never knowing
what you'd become.
If you'd make it out of your darkness,
if you'd ever be enough.

I sympathize, I do
but the cost was too high.
I loved you,
but at the expense of sacrificing myself,
I'd rather pay my dues
than lose myself saving you.

I wasn't your healer, I was your friend
I wasn't your savior, I was your lover
I could only do and give so much.

I hope my departure helped you see it wasn't personal, it was needed for us both; to be healthy versions of ourselves. I hope my absence brought you the space to be brave enough to discover yourself, love yourself, and unburden yourself so you can make enough room for someone to love you. I hope you finally do.

NOVEMBER 11, 2022
2:09 PM

My last relationship taught me a lot about myself. It taught me to never settle for comfort, especially when it comes in many disguises. It was the cleanse I needed to create boundaries. It taught me not everything stays the same, even when love is involved, it can get messy and things evolve. It taught me baggage needs to be left behind and healed before stepping into love with someone else. I couldn't give someone the healthy love I needed to give myself, first. My last relationship taught me not everyone I love will be a connection that lasts a lifetime, sometimes it's a reflection of who I am in that moment. A *tribute* to old versions of myself I needed to deal with and heal. Versions I needed to stop missing so I could transcend into a healthier version of myself; one I could love, one I could stop hiding from.

VOWS

I vow to embrace you tighter on your darker days but to hold you close to me every day after, too. I vow to pour into our cup as much as I pour into my own; to never drown or starve our love of the consistency it needs to keep growing. I vow to be your safe place to run to when you need protection; and your place of comfort when you need a quiet reflection. I vow to lift you on the days you find yourself dragging through. I vow to always remind you of your potential because you have shown me more than you can see. I vow to listen to you; I promise to hear you without making you feel like a hostage to your thoughts; because I know when they're dark, I can bring the light. I vow to never judge you and to always allow you to express yourself in the best way you choose. I vow to never deceive you, but instead, love you to my core, shamelessly because you are deserving of it. I vow to be your calm after every storm because our love will always stand the rain. I vow to always be the moon in your universe; to be your light as we both embody the essence of our union. I vow to love you and to always show you. I vow to never make you question it.

Love isn't enough. Love is what ignites the connection, it's not the only thing that keeps it flowing. Being committed. Being loyal. Being present. Being open. Being honest. Having patience. Having an open mind. Having respect. Showing support. Showing your appreciation. Showing the love you express, not just in the form of words. *Love isn't enough* to hold things together that were meant to break. *Love isn't enough* to make someone love you the same. *Love isn't enough* to change someone, to save them from themselves. *Love isn't enough* to make someone stay after every mistake. I wish love was enough because heartbreak would have no place in my life.

The toughest thing I was taught was; *love was never enough,* but that didn't mean I wouldn't stop loving — it didn't mean turn cold. It just meant I had to accept every lesson of love and free the love I lost; to welcome the healthy love I made no place for. *It was unhealthy of me to believe love was a superhero.*

You deserve to be happy. You deserve so much more than what you're settling for. You deserve to start over whenever you need to regroup. You deserve to find comfort in spaces that don't make you settle, instead, create a space for you to be free. You deserve to feel loved because you're worthy of the goodness you possess, too. You deserve to receive the same treatment you put into the universe because your effort is proof enough. You deserve to be accepted into the spaces you seek refuge in because you are worthy of peace. You deserve to breathe. You deserve to take a moment to focus, to recreate a new path to align your journey. **You are deserving of every step you take to find your way back to yourself.** You deserve to seek love within, don't let anyone allow you to believe you don't deserve it.

The *biggest hearts*
always find,
the *coldest* love.

I forgive myself for selfishly wanting to be loved, I gave the best parts of myself to those who never took me seriously. I should have given that love to myself, first.

UNNECESSARY SORROW

The love we shared seemed more like a business deal — *to heal each other*. We spent so much time filling each other's empty void, we didn't enjoy the company of each other. I was busy trying to be understood. I let you take your best shot with me. You were too busy trying to cope, to ever hold me the way I needed to be. We were never meant to become what we did. We could have saved ourselves the disappointment. We could have saved ourselves the lesson.

I don't have it in me, anymore,
to keep giving myself to those
who only disappoint me.
Who only ghost me.
Who only pretend to love me.

My heart doesn't have the strength
to keep opening it to those —
Who have no intention of nurturing it.
Who won't protect it.
Who will only end up harming it.

If you push me away,
stay away.
Don't try to rekindle
what you gave away,
what we had,
what we **created**.
I'm tired.
I refuse to keep giving my heart
to those who treat it like a burden.
I'm giving my love
to those who are worthy.
I'm giving my time
to those who value me.

Shame on me
for always seeing the best in you,
especially when you didn't deserve it.
When you took my heart
and completely shattered it.

Shame on me
for thinking this time could be different.

To not allow everyone to occupy my heart space that doesn't deserve a place. A connection ignited but sometimes it's a spark and the flame burns out; sometimes it's for a moment and the moment fades. Sometimes what we once were isn't what we are forever. To love and hold the capacity to set them free when they walk away-- without resentment, without the fear of feeling like I'll never return to myself again. *That is something I'm learning.*

If you **push me away**
I promise you,
I won't be here when you return.
I don't have what it takes
to keep *breaking my soul*
just to feel your love.

MEMORY LANE

I am so afraid of letting you go — to allow you to transcend without it feeling like an emptiness within me. I am so afraid of losing you, that your memory will somehow fade as time moves. I fear what it would feel like because I struggle to not remember the pain but to remember you without feeling the weight of losing you. I am so afraid of one day not remembering the way your smile lit up the room or the way your aura shined through. I am so afraid of unremembering you. I am so scared of unloving you.

HEARTBREAK 101

A broken heart won't be completely mended. It can't be fixed or replaced. You will remember every heartbreak. You will live with the loss. A healed heart will only create a shield for the suffering. A healed heart will only make you stronger in understanding loss. So, don't be so hard on yourself. It's okay to not be okay. It's okay to take as much time as you need to recover from what you're hurting from. It's okay to soak in the feeling a little longer than some might recommend. There's no time stamp on healing, there's no right or wrong route to take. You will heal on your own time. One thing that doesn't change is a damaged heart will always be broken because the people you love and the moments you lived will never be forgotten, you just meet a new version of yourself after each heartbreak.

DEAR YOU

Please, be *vulnerable*. Wear your heart on your sleeve. Don't allow anyone to diminish your worth or dim your potential. Being "too emotional" isn't a threat, it's a force not everyone can reckon with. It means you hold the capacity to bring a great deal of love and a great deal of pain, but with your soft heart, your intentions are pure. You're connected, aligned, and in tune. You can feel the energy shift in a crowded room. Your intuition speaks — you listen. You don't ignore the cycles of your emotions, even sadness has its right to occupy you, but never allow it to crowd you. You thrive when you're emotionally connected. You create connections through emotional intelligence, you're a sucker for those who share the same values — those who embrace your naked soul because they value you.

Sometimes you need to stop
watering dead plants
and start creating an environment
for new ones to grow within.

A good connection can be ruined over the simple fact that you miscommunicated or chose not to communicate.

A good connection can easily be lost because you choose to ghost instead of speaking about your fears, feelings, and intentions.

If you get lucky enough to create a beautiful friendship with someone and fall in love with them, don't let them go. That's the purest kind of love you'll find. Someone who's a friend to you, someone who loves you unconditionally, someone who falls in love with you too.

Healing the soul
is just as important
as healing the heart.

You may feel broken because a relationship ended, and you still hold feelings for it. You still love them and can't figure out how to not feel it. It's okay... the emotions remind you that your heart's big, even if you don't know it yet... that disconnection saved you.

It's not just about love. It's about someone who shows up for you. Someone who supports you. Someone who inspires you. Someone who pays attention to your love languages and shows you. Someone who loves you how they want to be loved and reciprocates it back to you.

Nothing is a waste of time
Not that 11-year friendship
Not that four-year relationship
Not that 20-year marriage

Step out the thought everyone is a mistake; it was
meant to happen that way. There's so much you
learned about yourself.
Thank them for showing you.

Dear self,

I'm proud of you because of your resilience. I'm proud of your ability to love through the darkest times and bring light even when you feel dimmed. I'm proud of your strength, not because of the weight you hold... but how you deal with every encounter. I'm proud of how you handle disappointment and don't disappear when you fear... you keep the faith and push through. I'm proud of your view of life and your ability to see every perspective, not just the one you feel fits best. I'm proud of the love you shower everyone with, even if they don't deserve it. I'm proud of the mistakes you turned into lessons learned. I'm proud of the journey, the fall, and getting back up. I'm proud you never once gave up, you never lost hope... you always fought to show your heart. I'm proud you never let this cold world break you.

I know *real love exists* because I am a mirror of it.

Writing my wrongs
and giving the apologies I never gave
because I was too selfishly deep into my pain,
I never acknowledged the disaster I brought too.

Two-sided story

I always chose to stay. So, shame on me. Shame on
me for letting you walk all over me. Shame on me
for letting you get into the depths of my soul that
no one has ever touched. Shame on me for putting
up with your mind games. Shame on me for
believing love would ever live within you.

Shame on you for always misleading me. Shame on
you for always making me feel we had a chance.
Shame on you for keeping me in your fantasy of
what we could be; when you had every
opportunity to set me free, you chose to let me
dream.

One thing I wished loved ones understood...

Take me as I am, don't assume or try to write me as the version you want me to be. Love me for who I am, not the potential friend or lover you wanted me to be. I've connected with many through forces that couldn't be denied but I felt we lost time because I wasn't recognized or felt on the level I was given. I learned to dim myself and become the version they wanted me to be because I never wanted to lose their love. I became codependent on their codependency without realizing it. I wish the ones who loved me would have loved me — the inner and every layer of me, so I didn't need to lose myself trying to be accepted by everyone who I loved.

Self-love is the most challenging chapter in your life to uncover. There are so many dimensions to loving every part of you. Accepting your flaws and how they tie into your beauty. Letting go of old habits that created toxic behavior, bringing in the new, the growth, and lastly, the love.

A **soulmate** isn't everyone you love throughout your life. A **soulmate** is someone who walks into your life and teaches you a love you never felt. It's a connection your heart can't deny. An unbreakable force. Not just a lover, a soulmate comes in all forms; cherish them all.

Stop the habit of overlooking when people hurt you. Whether it's a family member, friend, or lover. If they become toxic to your being, they shouldn't be kept. Love them from afar. Go ghost. Don't ever feel ashamed for choosing your sanity over hurting them.

Just because you 're born to love doesn't mean everyone is someone to love. Just because you have a connection doesn't mean your soulmates. Just because you gave all you had, and it didn't get reciprocated, doesn't mean give up. Love will find you when it's time.

I pray you all find someone
who matches your soul
the exact amount needed,
to fulfill that missing piece.
But before you find them,
I pray you find you.

Even as a work in progress, you should always think of yourself as the best version of yourself. Look at what you've become, and how far you've gotten, always be proud of your growth, and stop beating yourself up because you're not yet where you want to be.

Not every relationship can be "fixed" don't let anyone make you feel like you're wrong for walking away, instead of trying to save the love that's no longer love when it's become toxic. Some things aren't meant to be recovered.

I hope you always choose yourself if you're ever faced with that decision. I hope you always remember how important you are.

It's a goal to be with someone for the rest of your life. But make sure you're happy, secure, and loved unconditionally. Don't settle because you think it's too late; love has no timing, and your soulmate is out there and waiting to love you.

Being family doesn't mean you should allow toxicity. It doesn't give them a pass—it doesn't make them good people. You're not obligated to love your family just because you think you need to. I have friends who are more like family. Love who shows you they do too.

Let go of who hurts you.

I'm holding everyone who hurt me accountable for their toxicity until they can take accountability for their own behavior. I may have extended our time. I may have loved more. I may have created toxicity by staying, but they could have walked away, but they chose to play my heart to see how long I'd stay holding on.

We are all toxic to someone because we forced love when the chapter was written, when the book was already closed. Our intentions are pure, but the person and situation weren't right. We became toxic by chasing everything we wished to feel.

Keep your intentions pure and your soul at peace. *Be the vibe* only real ones crave.

If you push me away, you won't find yourself back in my life. I gave too many chances, too many times. I don't have it in me anymore, to fight, to keep rebuilding bridges that already burnt down.

I realized I couldn't be upset over holding someone to a higher standard when they never showed they were worthy. I expected more the many chances I gave. I tried to create this ideal love, friendship, and connection. I overlooked the signs that were written out for me. I didn't take accountability for the times I treated myself less just to be loved more by someone who couldn't love me halfheartedly. I never held anyone accountable for the times they hurt me when I kept taking them back, letting them get close when I should have left them in the dark. A lot of lost connections due to lack of support. Love was there but never strong enough to create an unbreakable bond. I had to work overtime to keep it up. I believed opposites attract, so I spent a lot of time trying to believe our differences we'd conquer, except they were just that, differences. I should have opened my eyes and saw everything clear as presented to me, but I saw with a different vision then, than I do now. I had to learn to be patient with myself and the real before it could ever get presented to me.

Find wholeness in your solitude
and I promise you won't attach loneliness
to weakness ever again.

I genuinely fell for someone when I wasn't searching for love, I was searching for peace. I was searching for myself and found a friend who became the love of my life. Sometimes you need to focus on growing yourself and you'll run into what's destined for you.

Some people don't deserve to know
the love after your growth, *close the book.*

My *depression* was a source of losing someone I loved... in the worst way. My depression came in like the waves of the ocean, loud but calming. I didn't notice I was experiencing something so daunting. I would smile throughout the day while being surrounded by people who lifted me and didn't know I was suffering. Until every moment alone I felt I was suffocating. The tears flowed without a source sometimes, and other times it was reliving the painful memories of what if and what already happened. I never felt more alone than I did in those moments. I couldn't find my path to healing because the emptiness was too crowded. I looked for a listening ear but my story was too played out for anyone to care. I couldn't be saved by anyone. I was looking to free myself from the sadness but there was no way out. I needed to feel to heal. I needed to embrace the part of my heart that will forever remain at loss, to finally be able to breathe again. Depression was the gift I needed to heal... not the kind of gift you unwrap and find happiness in, but the kind of gift you find at the end of a cycle of suffering... the wake-up call. The kind of gift you find after almost being destroyed. I think that should be celebrated. I survived.

Depression for me wasn't crying in bed all day, it was going to work, being with my loved ones... living my normal day-to-day life. Smiling and laughing... a lot of distractions. It wasn't until I was alone with my thoughts, they crept up. The times I feared the most were the most dangerous.

Heart to Hearts with my Inner child

I promised you I would never dig up what I made peace with, that once I healed from it I wouldn't let it harass me into being an afterthought. I knew the cost of dredging up the delicate moments but reflecting was better than suppressing. I know you felt like revisiting those broken moments would only revive those fires that couldn't be tamed. I know you felt I would sink back into that dark place. I know parts of you still live there. I want you to know I'm sorry, for dragging you through the misery like a bad song on repeat. I want you to know, that I always heard you, I just wasn't ready to listen. I want to apologize for neglecting you while I searched for ways to free myself, I should have catered to you, too. I ran from you instead of embracing you. I thought the trauma that surrounded my heart was me surviving my karma. I should have trusted you.

Forgiveness —

I don't seek it
I don't chase it
It doesn't live within closure.
The trauma won't fade
My heart will still ache.
Forgiveness isn't treasure
It's not a healing stone.

I could heal on my own
I didn't need their apologies
Their guilt and lies

To those who wronged me,
I forgive you —
for me,
for the sake of being free of you

forgiveness is reserved
for those
who deserve a second chance
not for those who abuse them

I believe I'm worthy of forgiveness
if I've ever wronged you,
I didn't just apologize...
I took accountability for my projections.
I never held grudges
and I never had ill intentions.
I won't ask for forgiveness,
I'm okay living with my decisions
my lessons.
I need to grace myself
with forgiveness,
to heal, to grow.

Projections —
I never meant to burden anyone with them
I never wanted to break anyone
I just wanted to be loved.
The trauma I didn't heal from
made me so hard to love.
I was blaming everyone
for my heartache.
It was my projections that broke everyone
It was my trauma
that continued to destroy me.

…I'm sorry

Twin flames are only healthy if you don't allow your flame to burn each other out. You both do the work needed to safekeep, heal, and maintain your fire. As long as you grow, inspire, and protect each other... otherwise, you will burnout and sometimes it's inevitable.

Maybe, I Love Too Hard

My **platforms**:

Instagram: Moonsoulchild
Twitter: Bymoonsoulchild
Tiktok: Bymoonsoulchild
Facebook: Moonsoulchild
Apple Music & Spotify: Moonsoulchild

Moonsoulchild.com

Printed in Great Britain
by Amazon

36162044R00131